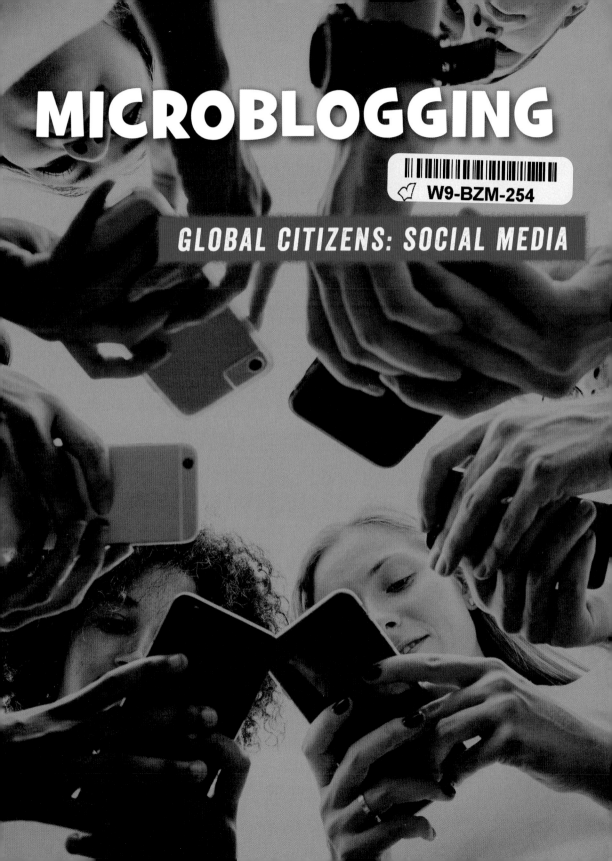

MICROBLOGGING

W9-BZM-254

GLOBAL CITIZENS: SOCIAL MEDIA

Published in the United States of America by Cherry Lake Publishing
Ann Arbor, Michigan
www.cherrylakepublishing.com

Content Adviser: Marcus Collins, MBA, Chief Consumer Connections Officer, Marketing Professor
Reading Adviser: Marla Conn MS, Ed., Literacy specialist, Read-Ability, Inc.

Photo Credits: © Rawpixel.com/Shutterstock.com, Cover, 1; © Benedix/Shutterstock.com, 5; © Bloomicon/Shutterstock.com, 6; © Kite_rin/Shutterstock.com, 8; © Vasin Lee/Shutterstock.com, 11; © Solomiya Malovana/Shutterstock.com, 13; © Twinsterphoto/Shutterstock.com, 14; © Rawpixel.com/Shutterstock.com, 17; © achinthamb/Shutterstock.com, 18; © Phonlamai Photo/Shutterstock.com, 19; © Dado Photos/Shutterstock.com, 20; © Kathy Hutchins/Shutterstock.com, 23; © Maxisport/Shutterstock.com, 25; © mentatdgt/Shutterstock.com, 26; © Sundry Photography/Shutterstock.com, 27; © Dmytro Zinkevych/Shutterstock.com, 28

Library of Congress Cataloging-in-Publication Data

Names: Orr, Tamra, author.
Title: Microblogging / Tamra B. Orr.
Description: [Ann Arbor, Michigan] : Cherry Lake Publishing, [2019] | Series: Global citizens: social media |
    Audience: Grade 4 to 6 | Includes bibliographical references and index.
Identifiers: LCCN 2018035582 | ISBN 9781534143050 (hardcover) | ISBN 9781534139619 (pbk.) |
    ISBN 9781534140813 (pdf) | ISBN 9781534142015 (hosted ebook)
Subjects: LCSH: Microblogs—Juvenile literature. | Online social networks—Juvenile literature.
Classification: LCC HM742 .O64 2019 | DDC 006.7/52—dc23
LC record available at https://lccn.loc.gov/2018035582

Cherry Lake Publishing would like to acknowledge the work of the Partnership for 21st Century Learning.
Please visit www.p21.org for more information.

Printed in the United States of America
Corporate Graphics

ABOUT THE AUTHOR

Tamra Orr is the author of more than 500 nonfiction books for readers of all ages. A graduate of Ball State University, she now lives in the Pacific Northwest with her family. When she isn't writing books, she is either camping, reading, or on the computer researching the latest topic.

TABLE OF CONTENTS

CHAPTER 1

History: The Drive to Communicate

Imagine you witnessed something amazing (or really lousy). What is the first thing you want to do? Chances are you want to tell someone. You want to share the details, describe the circumstances, and discuss the possibilities of what might happen next. That drive to communicate with others is part of what makes you human. Throughout time, people have shared their lives with others— from cave paintings to stories around the campfire to letters mailed across the country to Twitter and Instagram. Thanks to social media, people are more connected than ever.

Tumblr had almost 75,000 users sign up within two weeks of launching!

When Twitter launched in 2006, it was spelled "Twttr."

Enter PCs

The first home computer hit the market in the mid- to late 1970s. With computers came new modes of communication. Emails replaced letters. Instant messages replaced phone calls. You could chat with multiple people at once and have long conversations, without uttering a single word. You could write about your thoughts, opinions, and experiences online. Good-bye, journals. Hello, **blogs** and **microblogs**.

Timeline

1974–1977	Personal computers hit the market.
1998	Google is founded.
2004	Facebook launches.
2006	First **tweet** is sent.
2007	Tumblr launches.
	Cell phones become smartphones.
2010	Instagram launches.
2017	Twitter introduces 280-character tweets.
2018	Instagram introduces "Type" mode to Instagram Stories.

Unlike Twitter, Tumblr doesn't limit a user's post. However, most Tumblr users keep posts short, posting just an image and a brief caption.

Let's Be Friends

Social media revolutionized communication. People can now keep up with hundreds of their friends (or with people they wish were their friends). You know where they are, what they are doing, who they are with, when they got there, and why they went. Details are instantly accessible. Facebook, which was founded in 2004, connects you with everyone and gives you the chance to post pictures and messages. Twitter launched in 2006, followed shortly by Tumblr. Messages have grown shorter with each new type of **media**. Up until late 2017, Twitter only allowed 140 characters for its tweets. These messages are brief and to the point.

Posting on sites and platforms such as Twitter, Tumblr, Instagram, and Snapchat is known as microblogging. Similar to bloggers, microbloggers write what's on their mind, but they keep it brief and to the point. These sites allow you to write text, post pictures, upload videos and clips, send **GIFs**, and even link to another account. Posts on microblogs get right to the point. Posting could take as little time as snapping a photo. Although the world has changed dramatically in so many ways, the need for communication has not.

Developing Questions

In 2017, Twitter changed its policy and went from allowing 140 characters per tweet to 280. What is your opinion of this update? Do you think that part of Twitter's popularity is how short the messages have to be? Do you think Twitter made the right decision?

Opinions and facts are two very different types of statements. Facts can be proven (Abraham Lincoln was the country's 16th president). Opinions are feelings or beliefs about a subject (He was the best president we have ever had). Analyze your opinion about Twitter. How much of it is based on fact?

CHAPTER 2

Geography: The World and Microblogging

How often do you check your favorite social media site? According to studies, at least 6 out of 10 **millennials** are connected to a minimum of nine social platforms. The top microblogging platforms and sites used on a daily basis are Instagram, Twitter, Tumblr, Snapchat, and Weibo. You've most likely never heard of the last site. That's because it is a Chinese microblogging platform and is almost only accessible by people in China.

China

Millions of people throughout the world use Twitter. One-third of all users are in the United States (72.3 million). Japan is close behind, with almost 51 million users. Although the number should be zero in China since Twitter is banned, there are a reported 10 million Chinese users tweeting in secret using different hacking

Out of an estimated total of 1.5 billion daily active users on Facebook, about 546 million are in Asia.

methods. Free speech is limited in China, and the government controls the media. Currently, Facebook, Snapchat, Pinterest, Twitter, and YouTube are all blocked in China. Thousands of websites are blocked, and search results are **censored**.

Knowing that people needed a place to exercise free speech, Sina Corporation, a Chinese company, launched Sina Weibo in 2009. A cross between Facebook and Twitter, Weibo is a popular microblogging site in China. More than one-third of its people are active users. The site has even helped reunite missing kids with their parents and has inspired people to donate money to those in need. But users have also been known to post political opinions, something not allowed in China.

Why hasn't China shut the site down? It is simple: Weibo is growing so fast that not even the government can keep up with it. Xu Xiaoping, a microblogger with more than 1.5 million followers, said, "Weibo gives people power." Because of censorship, most Chinese trust the news they read on Weibo more than what they read in newspapers or hear on television.

To Ban or Not to Ban

Of course, China is not the only country that bans social media sites. Although their rules and laws do change, Turkey, North

Microblogging Mavens

If someone were to ask you which country has the most active users on Snapchat, Instagram, and Twitter, would you be surprised to learn that it's Saudi Arabia? According to a study, worldwide there are about 158 million users on Snapchat, more than 800 million postings on Instagram, and 336 million monthly Twitter users. Of those users, Saudi Arabians make up 12.9 million on Snapchat, 17.9 million on Instagram, and 17.3 million on Twitter!

About 58 percent of Tumblr users are from outside the United States.

Korea, Pakistan, Vietnam, Bangladesh, and Iran have blocked specific sites from their people. They do this for a number of reasons, but usually it's for political reasons. For instance, Turkey banned Twitter for two weeks in 2014 during political unrest.

Some countries work with microblogging sites to ban specific users from being visible to their citizens. Between late 2017 and early 2018, there were more than 1,700 Twitter accounts banned from being visible in seven countries: Russia, India, Brazil, Turkey, France, Germany, and the United Kingdom. Countries

There are far more Instagram users outside the United States, 80 percent, posting photos of themselves, their food, and what they're doing.

like North Korea have gone a step further and disconnected entirely from the World Wide Web, instead creating their own government-approved **intranet**.

A Site by Any Other Name

Twitter has had its name since 2007, but would you believe that this social media favorite was almost called FriendStalker or Twitch? After a few brainstorm sessions with his business partners, Twitter co-founder Jack Dorsey chose the name Twitter. His reason? Because of its dictionary definition: "a brief burst of unimportant information."

United States

In the United States, free speech is one of the most important and respected rights each person has. Being able to go online and post whatever is on your mind is protected by the nation's Bill of Rights. It means you can write your 280 characters or post a picture on any topic you want and not have to worry that it will be deleted or restricted because the government disagrees with it. However, keep in mind that each of these social media sites is owned by a business. So while you have free speech, there are rules to follow and manners to use when posting those micro messages.

Gathering and Evaluating Sources

One way to learn about two sides of an issue is through listening to or taking part in a debate. Each side of a debate presents strong points for or against an idea. It can present new concepts to you, or it can give you facts you might not have considered before.

Imagine listening to a debate on whether students should have access to social media in their classroom. Which side do you think you would agree with the most? What reasons would you want to add to one side of the discussion?

CHAPTER 3

Civics: Following the Rules and Regulations

Do you want to complain about your homework, vent about your brother, or get upset because you suspect your grandmother got you socks for your birthday again? You can immediately share your feelings online with the world. Microblogging platforms and sites provide a place for people to express themselves. But that does not mean people can say whatever they want, whenever they want, without facing consequences. Each platform and site has rules that have to be followed.

Facebook users have an average of 155 friends.

Twitter Tips

On Twitter, there is no regulation of content. No one has the job of sifting through the millions of tweets posted each day, looking for something out of line. However, if a Twitter user reports another user for violating one of Twitter's rules, an investigation begins. What is generally not allowed on Twitter?

- Pretending to be someone you aren't
- **Harassing** another person
- Posting private information without permission
- Posting more than 1,000 tweets a day (a day!)

Facebook deletes about 288,000 posts a month that don't follow its rules.

If Twitter determines you have done something that's not allowed, what happens next? It can do anything from limiting how many people can see your posts to banning you for life. In between are steps like hiding your profile or putting you in "time out" or read-only mode. This mode allows you to read posts, but not post or reply to anything for up to a week.

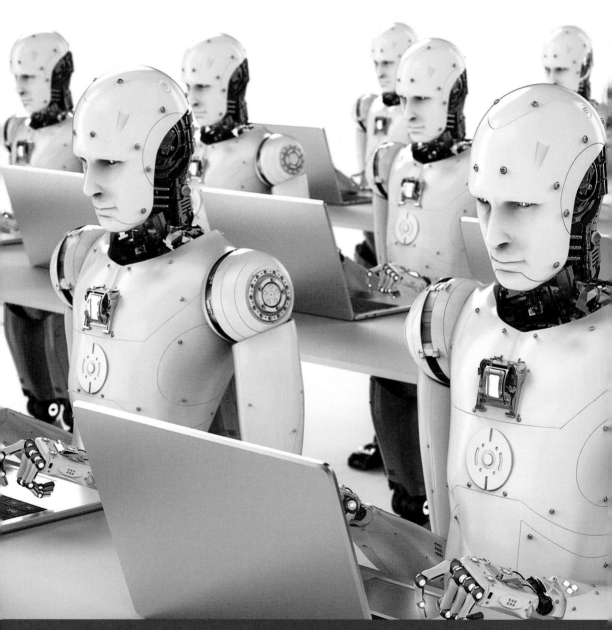

In 2018, there were about 70 million fake Twitter accounts that were suspended.

Instagram suspends accounts for a number of reasons, mainly to keep users safe and to get rid of fake accounts.

Facebook and Tumblr Advice

Finding the right balance between basic rights to free speech and rule-breaking is complicated for social media sites. Facebook is one site that has struggled with this. On one hand, Mark Zuckerberg, head of Facebook, has repeatedly said the company values freedom of speech. On the other hand, Facebook is a private company and can "police" posts and users as they see appropriate—which they have on multiple occasions. Any form of **hate speech** is banned, as are posts that directly threaten another person.

Tumblr does not tolerate the following: hurtful or unkind speech, threats of self-harm, content that is "sensitive" or "graphic," fake links, spam, harassment, or sharing of private information. Following the rules isn't the only thing that's important. Minding your online manners is as well. Certain behaviors are likely to lead to trouble. You shouldn't "troll" others or make fun of them. It's not worth losing your access to posting on social media.

Developing Claims and Using Evidence

If Twitter believes you are disobeying its rules, your account will be banned or suspended. It doesn't matter if you have zero followers or 20 million followers, or if you are a Nobel Peace Prize winner. In 2013, Nobel **laureate** Desmond Tutu joined Twitter only to find his account suspended hours later. Twitter thought his account was spam. The company later apologized.

Tutu isn't the only one who has had this happen. There have been other, far more controversial Twitter suspensions and bans. Using the internet and with adult supervision, research other people who have been banned from tweeting. Why were these people banned? How did they respond? Did they deserve to be banned? Use the information you find to form a statement answering these questions. Gather evidence to support the ideas in your claim.

CHAPTER 4

Economics: Influencing You and Your Money

Using social media is free. So how do social media companies make money? Look at the banners and scroll through a few posts—you'll see how! Facebook, Twitter, Tumblr, Instagram, and other microblogging sites depend heavily on the advertisements they display. Advertising budgets have doubled over the past few years, reaching into the billions of dollars. More than 90 percent of businesses say they will be increasing their budget again next year. But it isn't just the social media companies that are making money—the users are, too.

According to reports, Kylie Jenner makes about $1 million for every sponsored Instagram post!

#Influencer

If your best friend recommends a book to read or a song to listen to, are you more willing to do it? What if someone you barely know made the same suggestions? When you already know and trust someone, it is much easier to follow the advice that person gives. Ad agencies and marketing firms have known this for years. Thanks to sites like Instagram, companies use social media influencers to promote their services and products. Instagram is one of the biggest social media platforms for influencers to promote or market business and brands. This is also known as influencer marketing. In 2017, the platform had 12.9 million sponsored posts from influencers. It is estimated that in 2018, the market for influencer marketing will be $1.7 billion!

Social media influencers come in all shapes and sizes. They might be fitness enthusiasts, gamers, makeup gurus, fashion icons, athletes, or well-known celebrities. They most likely have thousands or even millions of followers. Companies often reach out to these experts and pay them (in free samples or a paycheck) to use, review, and comment on their brands and products. Payment varies from person to person, but about 84 percent of influencers

Communicating Conclusions

Before you read this book, how much did you know about microblogging? Is it something you were already doing or just getting started? Now that you know more about it, will it change how you write your next post? Share what you have learned with your friends. Look up social media sites other than the most popular ones, and see what you find. Also, take a closer look at some of the posts you've read. What can these posts show you about following the rules and minding your online manners? Share those thoughts with friends or family members.

After Kylie Jenner, the next highest paid Instagram influencers are Selena Gomez, who makes about $800,000 per sponsored post, and Cristiano Ronaldo, who makes about $750,000.

According to research, influencer marketing gained popularity from beauty, fashion, and fitness followers.

Facebook purchased Instagram for $715 million.
At the time, there were only 13 Instagram employees!

charge up to $250 for a single sponsored post. Some influencers, about 1 percent, are paid between $10,000 and $20,000 for one product post.

These influencers need to keep in mind the new ruling passed by the Federal Trade Commission (FTC). In 2017, the FTC ruled that users must clearly disclose if they are being paid to post. Most users add the FTC-approved hashtags, #ad or #sponsored, to their promoted posts. Despite this ruling, a report noted that 16 percent don't clearly reveal that their post was paid for.

According to studies, about 30 percent of people are more influenced and more likely to buy a product or service if it's recommended by a noncelebrity influencer.

Boost That Post

Not all microbloggers on social media platforms like Instagram and Twitter are influencers. But that doesn't mean they don't try to be. Many users pay Instagram, Twitter, and Facebook to help them reach a wider audience and grow their followers. Users can pay as little as $5 to as much as their budget allows.

Microblogging is a style of reaching out to others. It can share good and bad news. It can ask people to take an action. It allows you to send a message to companies, network with your community, and connect to the world. It fills that very basic human need to communicate—even if you have to count your characters and leave out the adjectives in the process.

Taking Informed Action

Do you mainly microblog to chat with friends or catch up on each other's lives? Why not give some thought to microblogging to help a cause? There are a number of local, state, and national organizations that could use your help, including those dealing with disabilities (#wheelchairlife), racial issues (#blacklivesmatter), and natural disasters (#crisiscommons). Find out what other causes are active in your area and look into getting involved.

Think About It

A study showed that people from different generations use the internet in dramatically different ways. For example, people between the ages of 18 and 24 used the internet far more for social networking, video sharing, and photo sharing than those in the older generations. Also, 39.1 percent of the youngest group went online for microblogging, while only 15.8 percent of those 55 and older did. Why do you think this is the case? Research this topic further using the internet and your local library. Use the information you find to support your argument.

For More Information

FURTHER READING

Furgang, Adam. *Snap and Share: Exploring the Potential of Instagram and Other Photo and Video Apps.* New York: Rosen Publishing, 2015.

Henneberg, Susan. *Twitter Safety and Privacy: A Guide to Microblogging.* New York: Rosen Central, 2014.

Kenney, Karen Latchana. *David Karp: The Mastermind Behind Tumblr.* Minneapolis: Lerner Publications, 2013.

Orr, Tamra. *Tweeting with a Purpose.* New York: Rosen Central, 2018.

Wilkinson, Colin. *Twitter and Microblogging: Instant Communication with 140 Characters or Less.* New York: Rosen Central, 2012.

WEBSITES

Safety Net Kids—Staying Safe Online
www.safetynetkids.org.uk/personal-safety/staying-safe-online
Learn about how you can stay safe online.

Lifewire—What Is Microblogging
www.lifewire.com/what-is-microblogging-3486200
Read about microblogging and see some examples.

GLOSSARY

blogs (BLAWGZ) short for weblogs; online diaries or journals

censored (SEN-surd) officially removed of content considered to be offensive

GIFs (GIFS) image file formats; stands for "graphic interchange format"

harassing (huh-RAS-ing) bothering or attacking another person

hate speech (HAYT SPEECH) direct attacks on people based on their race, ethnicity, nationality, religion, gender, sexual orientation, or disability

intranet (IN-truh-net) a local or restricted communications network

laureate (LAWR-ee-it) someone who receives an honor or is recognized for an important achievement

media (MEE-dee-uh) a method of communication between people, such as a newspaper

microblogs (MYE-kroh-blawgz) very brief posts on social media sites

millennials (muh-LEN-ee-uhlz) people born in the 1980s or 1990s

tweet (TWEET) a post on the social media website Twitter

INDEX

[21ST CENTURY SKILLS LIBRARY]